MY LIFE TILL 16TH

Dirgh Gandhi

BLUEROSE PUBLISHERS
India | U.K.

Copyright © Dirgh Gandhi 2024

All rights reserved by author. No part of this publication may be reproduced, stored in a retrieval system or transmitted in any form or by any means, electronic, mechanical, photocopying, recording or otherwise, without the prior permission of the author. Although every precaution has been taken to verify the accuracy of the information contained herein, the publisher assume no responsibility for any errors or omissions. No liability is assumed for damages that may result from the use of information contained within.

BlueRose Publishers takes no responsibility for any damages, losses, or liabilities that may arise from the use or misuse of the information, products, or services provided in this publication.

For permissions requests or inquiries regarding this publication, please contact:

BLUEROSE PUBLISHERS
www.BlueRoseONE.com
info@bluerosepublishers.com
+91 8882 898 898
+4407342408967

ISBN: 978-93-5989-529-1

Cover design: Tahira
Typesetting: Tanya Raj Upadhyay

First Edition: January 2024

My life till 16th

CHAPTERS :-

Introduction

Chapter 1 :- crush

Chapter 2 :- money can buy happiness

Chapter 3 :- love

Chapter 4 :- family and friends

This is to inform
You in right side

The story will be
Continue .

In the left side I have
Choose activities
Or photos or screenshot
Of the truth or fact

Note

All the Characters mentioned in my book are real and alive I have consulted the in dividual Whosenames I have Written, some of the names are nick names or not the real names due to privacy reasons. The book is based on my real life Situation and experience I apologize to people Whose Feelings are hurt Cause I have used cursed Words regarding them and GF also Last but not least me DIRGH Gandhi hopes this Succeds than I Will definitely think of Writing another one, I hope you enjoy it

Viața este totul
despre suișuri și jos.

Translate it

INTRODUCTION

Hello I am Gandhi and this is my story Aree don't go i am not mahatma Gandhi I am dirgh gandhi I am writing this book because I want to tell lots of things of my life. first of all my English is not good It means grammatical mistake . That's why I am writing this book in hindi but words is in English it means hinglish . this is all about my life till 16th up and downs related to my Crush ,dream, mom ,dad ,brother, teacher, money, family, drama and many more. This book I am writing in a way of diary. The chapters will be small like one or two pages and this book will be also small but I bet you that you will enjoy it.

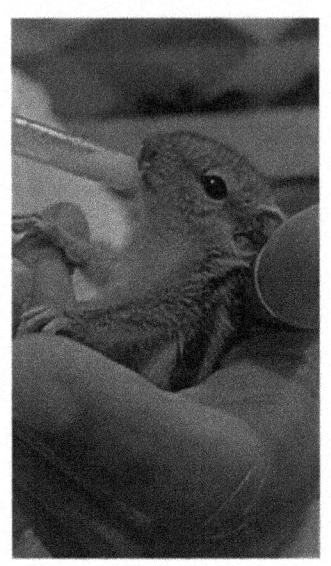

This is my pet squirrel

At the end of this book, let's start again. Hello. I am dirgh Gandhi and this is my story. I am Gujarati belonging to Ahmedabad kem cho. Don't say not in majama. Who am I not enough to earn money can't roast many peoples and many more but I am good to have some nice friends. I know I am going of the topic but sometimes I feel alone that's why I like to watch Movies alone and the all thing I ask to papa he give me like PS4 mobile phone s22 ,watch and many more let's here a joke. What did the pig say on a hot day? I am bacon I know it's not funny

It's me

A.K.A DIRGH GANDHI

CHAPTER -1- CRUSH

I have lots of Crush but one of tuition one I will remember every time I am not going direct to point let's start with my first Crush. What is Crush from my side that is one feeling about which you are not sure but you love her as 65% Crush are like which If you propose her and she accepts than your luck neither you will be a brother or best friend and that is okay. I think that Crush is a different world and love is a different world Crush aapko apni ungaliyon mein nachaati hai aur love Hai To Ek Din tutna Hai yah Pyar Hota Hi aisa hai Mil Gaya to theek

Nahin to Puri jindagi Kabir Singh bante Rah Jaenge vah ladki ko to theek dusra mil Jaega but Ham Rote Rah Jaenge uski Yad mein. yah Duniya Pyar Ko Kabhi acche najrein se nahin Dekhti vah paise ko Dekhti hai jo ladki ke liye to Achcha hai per ladkon ke liye sabse Bura hota hai use Waqt hai ki ladke bahut paise nahi Kama Sakte paise ke saath- saath Khandan ka bhi mahatva Hota Hai Achcha Khandan Nahin Hua to ? to aapko Sabko pata hai kya hota hai? Bollywood give us happy ending for love stories, but it's not correct at all. There are some with Heart break movies. Like tadap When I was seeing Tadap mere ko laga ke father is a villain but no the lady was the

Who was your
First, second
And third
Crush

1.

2.

3.

main villain. She was playing with him. In titanic jack die To save rose and what happened next? Rose married with a man named calvert and they have three children. Romeo and Juliet unke Parivar Kabhi Nahin Mane last end Mein dono sath mein Mar Gaye this was from Hollywood and one from Bollywood I have talked a lot about crush and gone of the topic. Chalo mere pahle Crush per Aate Hain She was asshka Main Usko first standard se Pasand Karta Tha but you know Crush can be change second Crush was Jacqueline mere ko pata hai aukat se bahar main ja raha hoon. Ek Ladki Thi megha Naam Ki pata nahin Kyon mere ko Uske naam ke sath chidhate

Why she / he Was your First Second and third Crush

Reasons :-

1.

2.

3.

the mere ko vo bilkul bhi acchi Nahin lagti thi. Mere ko uske upar kabhi kabhi matlab Kabhi Crush Aaya hee Nahin I dont like her at all. But some boys and girls chidhate the after all one day at age of 11 or 10. She propose me and I say no and I maked her sister you don't know what demand she put. you will not talk with girls And lots of things after agreeing these all tell me Yes I said you are mad pagal hai aur Maine Na Keh Di yaar main flutter boy hu aur usko Tum kah rahe ho ladki ke sath baat mat karo seriously girls mere ko kabhi bhi society wali ladkiyon per Crush Aaya hi Nahin bahut Logon per Crush aaya but society wali ladkiyo

Who was your
First actor
Or actress
Crush

Your

1.

Your best friend

1.

Not at all.
Let's come to tuition crush name dharini surname. I can't tell yaar bolne Mein taklif hota hai isliye. Jab 4 standard Mein Tha tab Tution joined kiya tha Aur usne Pahle Se Hi.usi Waqt crush ke bare mein Kuchh pata nahin tha. 5th ke baad pata chala what is Crush after all I didn't tell my feelings to her jab tak mere dost ne yah Kand nahin kiya tha Ek Din Maine usko kaha ke Uske Dost Ko BataDe majak (joke) mein aur usne sahi mein kah diya after one day tution ex student message me .ke you have crush on dharini. I say yes, aise mistake life mein kabhi mat karna 2 din baad dharini ka message aaya first of All

Fact

" Life mein kya kya karna padta hai Ek Ladki Ko patane ke liye aur jab aapane yah Baat aapke dost ko kah Di to samajh lo vah Baat ab aapki aur aapke dost ke bich Ki Nahin Hai Sabke bich ki hai.Kyunki vah Harami to Sabko Bata hi dega."

I was thinking that my number is leak because use maheene bahut message aa rahe the un logo se jinko, maine number hi nahi diya. aaaaaaa off topic point per Aate Hain usne bola call kar and I was thinking that konsi ladki call ke liye message karti hai

To maine obviously Ek Bahana Diya I am eating food. She said afterwards call me when you are free. I said OK thodi der ke baad Maine usko phone kiya usne uthaya Zindagi mei Maine pahli bar uske sath ek ghante tak Baat kee Mera ek dost hai usne bola tha ki Piche mat pad main Kaha manne wala tha . You know just Gandhi things usne bola (dharini) vah Bachpan se girls school mein padhati hai is Waqt mere ko Idea agaya

Kisi ladki or ladke par tumko Crush aaya hai
In family function
Without knowing her/his names
How many times

Ans

gaya tha vah kya Kahana chahti hai maine usko pocha You know for clarification boys things. She said she is a biosexual. Who don't know bisexual kya hota hai let me explain bisexual means sexually or romantically attracted to both men and women or to more than one sex or gender Pura Google se chhapa Mara hai. But in Simple words usko Male bhi pasand hai aur female bhee Aur aajkal yah sab normal Hai I can't do anything in this or usne. Fir Kuchh gine chune logon ko hi bataya tha. Aur Main best friend ban gaya just I tried my best Achcha tab Nahin Laga Jab usne block kar diya.Use Waqt dost ki Yad a rahi thi mere ko aur block kiya

How is your Parents Like:-

A- cool

B- streak

C- medium

D- none of these

bhi kab ek mahine aur do mahine Baat usne Kiya . she unblock Me afterwards by giving a useless reason ke Puri conversation Jo use Din hui thi Ham donon ke bich main aapko likh ke dikhata Hoon I put a story on whatsapp of my photo. She shared a Pink heart after this I type dharini after so long time. She reply. Yeah I had to block you because of some personal issue. Sorry, if you are mad first of all how I will get mad, I can't understood.Then I reply which personal issue and you want to block me again don't message me yaar likhna padta hai.Bura Lagta Hai Koi block kar de to she said are I had my cousins over here is my big brother he came from Jaipur okay, and he was

Have you ever Propose your Crush?

Yes :-
No :-

And what was his/her Ans:-

continuously asking for my phone and if he had saw our chats, I would be gone. So without any saying I had to block you.I tell okay and she didn't block me till now or Hum To Pagal Hai Yeh reason sunkar.Who knows the reason was truth or false? Okay To Kuchh gine chune Logon Ko usne bataya hai to I have taken permission from Dharni to write about her and second thing.Now me and dharini is a nice good friends.like Instagram per Main Usko reels share karta hun vah mere ko reels share Karti Hai Meri birthday party mein I Thi aur abhi 10th Mein Na Hoti to Aur Bhi Bahar Milte Aur vah dost ne Jo bola tha vah. I think galat hi bola tha mere ko Nahin

Which song do
You dedicate
To your First
Crush?

And why
:-

Lagta ki vah Kuchh Lagu hota hai Iske upar.like I said crush to Aati Rahegi aur jaati RahegiVah To Apne Upar hota hai yah kaun si Crush ko Humko select karna hai Vahi ek chij hai jo Ham kar sakte hain bahut dusri dusri bhi hoti hai, but yah chij Ham Dil Se Karte Hain Aur Dil Se Usko Fir Hata bhi Dete Hain Okay to Bus Itna Hi Tha Crush Mein move Tu next chapter

Chapter-2- money can buy happiness

Crush wale chapter Ki Tarah Bada To Nahin Hoga but maja to aaega. Yes, I believe that Money can buy happiness because without money in this earth there is nothing free . paise Se Hee Sab Kuch Hai Paise Ke Bina Kuchh Bhi Nahin Hai Paisa Hai To Ijjat Hai Paisa Nahin to vah bhi nahin oxygen is also not free Jab aap ventilator per Hote Ho tab Aapko oxygen ki bhi jarurat hoti hai aur use Waqt Hospital wale bahut charge karte hain oxygen ke liye Kuchh log bolenge ki Mom Ki feelings aur papa ki feelings same

What do you
Think money
Is everything or not
I want your
Opinion

Ans

time vah bhi free Nahin Hoti Hai Vah bhi paise per a Jaati Hai Jab Chhote the tab Rote the tab Mummy Give me a chocolate not my parents do this everyone's do this Any few are thinking Kaisa ladka hai apne mummy or papa ko bhi paise se compare kar raha hai to this idea has been given by my mother so mere ko judge mat karo. Now a days girls ask expensive things when we are in a relationship. That's why for me love is a materialistic, you know in last end of Race 2 when there is nothing with John Abraham how Jacqueline change the party. money is everything just Paisa Sab ke pass hota to Garibi Nahin Hoti no poverty but Kya Karen

What is your Favorite currency Not from your Country ?

Your :-

Ans

Best friend:-

Ans

Paisa To Har EK Desh Mein alag alag tarike se hai bahut Sare movies aur web series mein dikhaya Hai Paisa aa jata hai to ghamand aa Jata Hai like example taaja Khabar, Baazaar and The Wolf of the Wall Street and kuttey also Paisa Hai To Bhagwan Hai. Nahin to Kaha Sab Kuchh hai? Paisa Hai To festival (tehvaar) hai. Paisa Insan ke pass Limited Rahana chahie Nahin to Income Tax ki raid bhee padh sakti hai Jab Paisa Itna mahatva nahin karta to Kyon ladkiyan divorce ke Waqt Itna Paisa mangti hai I know Government schools are there but you know Indian government school, it's not that much good. Jab yah sirf kagaj ka tukra hai aur tumhari life ko decide kar raha hai

Your favorite Money song

My :- Paisa Hai toh

Your :-

Your best Friend :-

to aap Logon Ko samajh Jana chahie uska Life Mein Kitna Jyada importance hai. Mahabharat bhi paise ke hisab se hui thi Jab kaurav ko pandavon ko Kuchh Jameen ka tukra bhi nahin dena tha. Lord Krishna ask for 5 village but kaurav didn't give so that's why the battle took place . land is equal to money All boys think that girls only want money and if the boys had money he can get any girl whom he like, sometimes some girls were like this but not all girls like money the greatest importance of money is time but boys can't understand this but ab sahi hai ki girl bhi paise kee Pass Jaati Hai that's all for this chapter let's move to next chapter.

Chapter -3- love

Ok! Ok! There is a difference between love and crush, crush are temporary. But love is permanent and there is not one type of love only of GF, Pyar maa ka bhi Hota Hai ,Papa ka bhi hota hai See I respect my parents and they are very cool parents like kal maine bola Mere papa ko Ke Mere science Mein acche marks nahi aayega bahut kam, aree wapis off topic baar baar of topic Jata rahata hun main to ignore it please okay. Pyar Ek Bar hota hai to use nibhana bahut jaruri hai.Tumne usko acchi tarike se nahin nibhaya to vah jaldi Tut bhi sakta hai Chahe vah family ka ho ya Gf ka ho vah jaldi Tuti

Who was your true love?

:-

jata hai ghar wala Divorce Tak Jata Hai GF wala to Ek temporary hota hai jaldi Tut jaega. Dard to donon Mein same hi hota hai. mere ko Pyar Saccha wala Ek Bar Hua Hai Aur Dard Bhi hua hai my fourth GF Zana It's not a real name because for privacy issues But the word start with Z and the meaning of this name and her name is similar She was my 4th gf and I love her like she was my first. I love to talk with her, fight with her and more with her. time ka pata He nahi chalta tha baat baat aur sirf baat karte Rehte the but that has gone. She broke up with me and main Kabhi move on nahi kar Paya .Aaj Bhi Main use dekhta hoon. Aur Pyaar Vaisa hi a jata hai main kuch nahi kar

Fact

" Insan ko kabhi
Pyar karna hi
Nahin chahia "

Find your love
If you think Samne
Wala app ko Pyar karta
Hai aur aapke sath
Time spend karna usko
Achcha Lagta Hai
Nahin to tel peene Jaaye

sakta to sirf Baitha rahata hun you don't know But whom I love they always go .everyone everyone means everyone like my all pets Woh Ek Do mahine Mein Mar Gaye Mere Papa ok to papa ko bhi kuch hua hai We will talk about on family topic isliye maine Apna khud ka space dhundh liya hai. Not everyone knows My space to see movies alone. Not alone I have one basically one partner my water bottle because no one comes with me. Okay thoda sa depress Ho Gaya let change the topic I know ma off topic Jata hu Aage ka chapter bol diya hai Just ignore it. I had said only my 4th GF zana Whom I love most but Kuch Din Pehle Mujhe Pata Chala 8th

One day before break up

standard Mein Aur zana 4th month ka relationship tha. Okay 4 months Mein Mujhe Itna Pyar Ho Gaya usse.
usne Aisi aisi baten ki Ke Pyar Ho Gaya Dard hota hai mujhe app side mein screenshot dekh sakte ho b******* Pardon my language but sali mere mind ko vash kar diya tha nagin thi nagin so Basically Maine Uske baare mein achha achha hi likhane wala tha, but my friend Vishwa.s , vishwa p.y aur Heer ine Logon Ne bola. She was just playing with me. Ok guys. You don't know but in 8th standard. I was very popular guy she wants to be popular girl That's why she came into relationship to be popular after knowing this I was shocked. You can

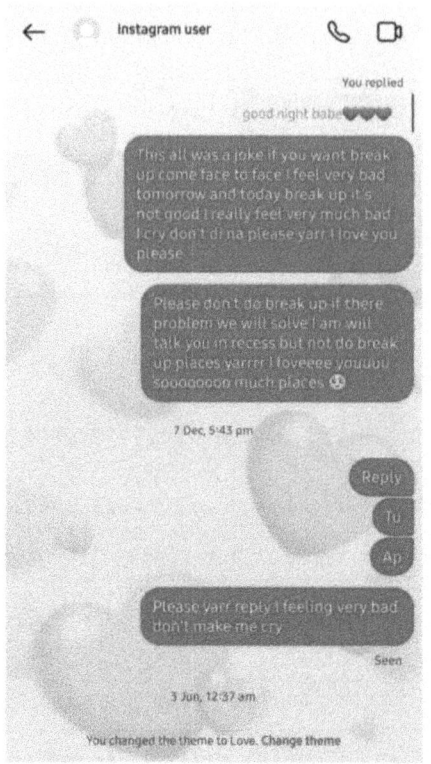

Uske Samne Sab Sigma Sigma Nikal Gaya

see the screenshot of ,our breakup was a mutual understanding at the last she Said that I will always love you. Now when I know everything I feel use and the point is when zana propose me after 2 days. She said it was a dare and if you want to continue the relationship we can and I was fool who tell yes to continue the relationship now just go to hell zana And move on to next topic. Ok. So in love chapter. I want to include my all ex topic because it's very interesting.

Okay. So first I was studying in ANM (Anand Niketan) and when I change the school there was lockdown going on

Someone's parents has come to school to complaint about you ?

Yes :-

No :-

Online classes and more if you are student, you know everything what was done in locked down. Okay class was going online And offline .class started who wants to come they can come because the government had announce if parents give permission They will come online and offline both classes will be able to attend both. I like to go okay. I want to go I meet Bansari we become nice friends and soyam. Also we talk in call more.There was bansari best friend pisha who also was in call I can describe pisha in one word it is play girl.She propose me and I tell yes, she was third GF after pisha there was zana come ok.Pisha is not a real name. I have just change the first

Who was your first second and third girlfriend or boyfriend?

1

2

3

aur Kabhi Bani aur bana hi Nahin

letter. We started talking in call and I was thinking she is okay Okay, nice and more but tum Jise sochte Ho waisa Kabhi hota nahi Yeh point hai. Okay yaar main bahut ok Bolta Hoon so usko bhi ignore karo Ok. So one day, I called pisha and her mother pick up call. I was like ok ok, I talk to her mother and told a lie that I want notes ,after 10-20 minutes from another number one call came to my phone and it was her father uska Baap Is Duniya ka sabse bada Pagal aadami Hai Sala school mein aa gaya tha and Bol Raha Tha Main uski ladki ko harass karta hoon. Matlab kuch bhi uska Baap School Mein Aaya Tha Ek reason se aap sunoge to you will like what the hack

What would you do if you were in my position?

Ans

just I said, we have a mutual friend Bansari so after art lecture over Main Aur Bansari No spill Pot ko dhone gaye the so just we were playing with water pisha jumped between our water playing so main thoda Baki Rehne Walo Main Nahi Hoon so Maine uske upar Pani fenka aur usne Wapas Mujh Par Pani fenka.Basically we played Holi in school. She complaint to her music teacher uske sath Mera 36 ka aankada hai. So Maine toh uske mu pe bola If you don't believe me, then check CCTV camera to music teacher that day all over Happy Ending but dusre Din on her birthday her father came like classroom ke door ke bahar Khada Rah apni beti ko bulaya uska

First read this page and answer my question kitni baar jhoot bola hai ?

Ans

usko bola kaun hai? Woh Ladka usne Meri Taraf Ishara Kiya aur mere ko bulaya, life mein first time Koi Pehli Baar family member. Aaya tha mere school life mein till 7th Meri Kisi Se fatati Nahin Hai Sirf Mere Papa aur mummy Ke Siva usne Bulaya main Toh Uske pass gaya My class teacher of 7 she said wait don't go after 5 minute. I was Called to principal room. He was telling this boy is harassing my daughter throwing water on her and calling her again and again and harassing her main mere mind main (kuch bhi kuch bhi.)Principal mam told me this is right or wrong. So I told mam first of all she threw water on Me if you can't believe check camera what is your favourite love song ?

My :- Aaj ke baad
The fact is I was in Aaj ke baad song

Your :-

second. I told little bit lie that I don't know her daughter properly also and at that time I was new student in school. So I told in zoom meeting if anyone can give me his or her number because I want notes so thats all I tell to principal mam. principal mam, believe me and uska Baap mere se argument Mein Har Gaya Aaj Tak koi bhi mere sath argument Mein Jeet Nahin Paya Hai. my winning ratio in argument is 80% jhooth Aisa bolo Ke Samne Wale Ko yakin Ho Jaaye Apne Andar Itna confidence hona chahiye aur Jitna Jhooth bolo na 10% Sahi Hona chahie like Mera tha CCTV wala tha So I tell to my mama. This was happened in school and mama tells

Till now how many girlfriends do you have or boyfriends?

Ans

OK I will talk to papa and he told to papa. My phone was Ban for a month. That's all my papa get understand. It was not my mistake bus Yahi Thi Meri ex ke story.

My current love live status is not single I am in a relationship with the beautiful girl her name. I can't tell because she said no, that's why after 7 month. I am in a relationship basically, but there is a problem she is my GF but her best friend is zana Who is My ex . soyam is my best friend and she is his ex Bahut lafada hai. I know but we both are happy I propose her and she said yes after one day mere ko pata nahi chal raha hai Ki Itna Bura Sapna aata hai your favourite love movie ?

My :- Ajab Prem Ki Ghazab Kahani

Your :-

yaar bol bhi nahi sakta sorry for that Okay, so I have not tell you about my first gf and second GF my total GF is five I know it's sounds odd ignore it akku she was my first GF in class 1 I saw her and first it was a new school. Ok. So I have saw her first time really one word came out from my mouth awesome. She was really cool bhai baat Hi mat karo woh kya thi,In class 5th she propose me wait if you are getting confusing chapter 1 you have said that dharini was your crush and your friend tell to her friend so basically I had crush on dharini. in 5th class But my friend told to her friend in eight. Ok, so she propose me (akku) not me in class 5th. I was shy but now

What would you choose if I give you or someone else love or money?

:- love
:- Money
Why reason
Ans

you can't imagine how am I okay continue to 6th. in 6th me and her was very close. But what to say Corona came, online class started and unfortunately I have to leave school. Okay, please don't think yaar Playboy have school leave karne ke sath dusri GF Bana Di so it was Corona that's why I didn't get admission to another school. So I join new school after 1 year get over. It's very sad. So me and akku broke up. I was not happy seriously. It was my first but it not get that's much sad In compare of zana okay, so that's was my first GF story second remaining only one. And akku is not a real name.
Mandira ji han ji, she was second

here, I don't have any type of questions. So I put my squirrels photo.

Mandira and we have lot of culture different. It doesn't matter if these was not happened. She was from Kolkata and I am Gujarati you know already this. when she came to Gujarat we were on relationship, but she gone back to Kolkata for lifetime and someone has said long distance never work It's true. We started talking less on call and chats and one day. I told her it's over buss . This was my love life till today. Sometimes I talk with Akku on chats with Mandira no contact with pisha many times than zana she is ignoring me And Mandira is a real name.And the one her name. I can't tell she always talk with me. I think I should rate 10 out of dash

So till now I have five girlfriends which story do you feel it was very sad ?

Ans

that how much I loved them.

first akku 6 out of 10

second Mandira 4 out of 10

third pisha 2 out of 10

fourth Zana 9 out of 10

last unknown 7 out of 10

I know Aise Kisi Ko rating Nahin Dena chahie but de raha hun main that's all let's move to next chapter.

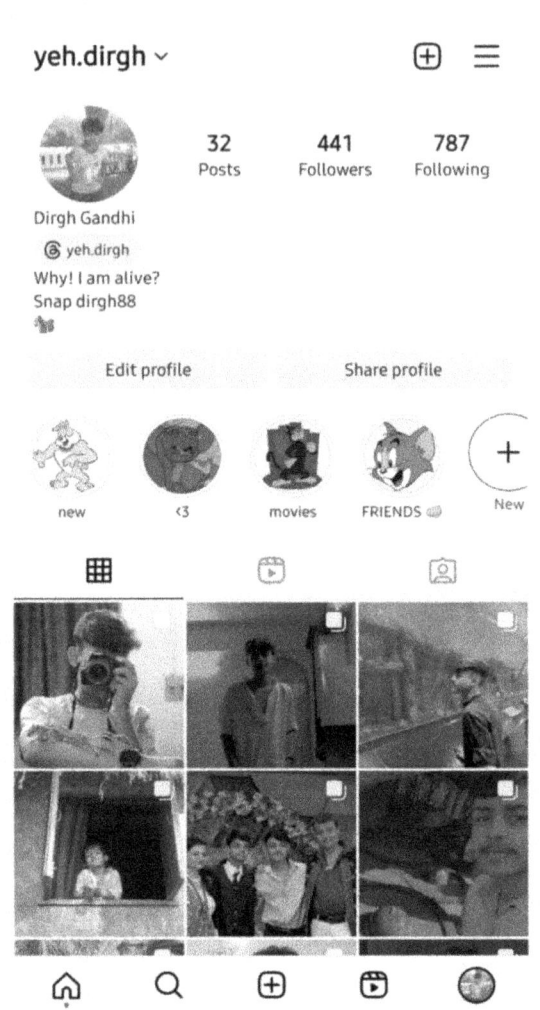

This is my Instagram ID if you have any question just send me a message.

Like ma Tu yeh chapter over kar ne Vala tha but Just in the last few days something happened with me that I have to tell you guys like I was doing my favorite jobs Back hypocrisy it's means ma Peeth Piche Baat Kar raha tha of zana I told everyone two things like zana done this with me and etc etc and Second there is my friend Jo yah sari khabren late Hain so one news I get zana has crush on kathan and kathan is my nice friend Basically Mere Piche exam ke Waqt vahi baith ta tha hai aur mera aur uska banta hai Kyunki anime Ham donon ko bahut pasand hai vo topper hai I was really shocked after hearing the news that zana has crush on kathan like Maine anime Mein Ek Hi Dekha Tha fir usne mere ko introduce karaya anime community sa to aap Soch sakte ho ki vo mera Kitna Achcha dost ho sakta hai Aur exam mein

my favorite top 3 anime are:-
1. Death note
2. Jujutsu kaisen
3. Demon slayer
Your :-

main uske hisab Se Hi pass hota hun. I told everything to kathan that zana is like this and etc etc Kyunki usko zana acchi Na Lage because somewhere I feel I like zana the fact is I love her not likeI know tum log soch rahe ho isliye to Aur Ek Ladki Ko Pata Diya but one month ke bada Maine Breakup kar liya Kyunki mere ko Achcha Nahin lag raha tha Kuchh be Nahin Tha Jaise zana ke sath Tha maine uska dil dukhaya hai mere fifth girlfriend and I am really fell sorry for her after my 16th birthday party I can't even talk with her I tell to her we are nice best friends we can be friends she was crying what a shame dirgh gandhi what a shame ok so kathan told me I am not telling her yes maybe kathan said Jab vah mere ko propose Karegi tab main sochunga. All ok So there is some Stomach problem. That's why I am

Mini me

sitting in classroom in our school boys go downstairs and girls stay on floor zana entered in classroom and tell me don't spread Rumor about me Aur use Samay main Kuchh bolane ja raha tha usse pahle vah Chali gai I was like which one there are two I have tell everyone about you which one you talking about after all I never tell anybody about her and I feel like she was talking about kathan one's who know I think vo Sabko Jhooth kah rahi hai ki mere ko dirgh Pasand Nahin Hai like covering herself Because usko pata hai ki main yah sari chij Mein Pad Gaya to main padhaai Mein Dhyan Nahin dunga now this thing god knows I think because at the time of break up we both decided to leave each Other because school mein relationship Pakda ja raha tha I would like to over this There is something to Continue here I want

Fact

" peeth Piche Itni sari Baat Nahin Karni chahie Jaise Maine ki use Waqt Ke bad ab tak Maine Baat Nahin Ki Peeth Piche" to tell you more about me It is not related to love but I am continue in here because I don't want to make an another chapter for this like dirgh gandhi Kyu yeh book ko likh raha hai Mere ko bhi nahin Pata I think Meri feelings batane ke liye Ja Mere Pass Kuchh Karne Ko Nahin Hai main sirf Yahi Baitha hun, aur yah likhate ja raha hun likhate ja raha hun likhate ja raha hun life mein kya ho raha hai mere ko usse Kuchh Lena Dena Nahin Hai Jo Insan padh bhi acche se Nahin Sakta Hai Khel bhi acche se nahin sakta hai sirf tv. Aur phone Dekhta rahata Hai Uska Sapna kya hai ek actor Banna Ek nice director usko to log nakama hii samjhenge I just want to read Manga I just want to watch movies first day first show or third day log mere ko Kahate Akele picture Dekhne Mein Kya maja hai main Kah Raha Hun Akele Dekhne Mein hi vah Maja hai jo

THE DIRGH GANDHI SHOW

Sath Dekhne Mein Nahin Koi vah picture ko to judge Nahin karega jaise Humko Karte Hain .Thoda depressing Ho Gaya Main Usko over karna chahta hun You know, what was my proud moment? it was my old School Anand Niketan there was night stay and aapko Pata Hai night stay Kaise hote hain. majedar Hote Hain so that day I perform anchoring I know my friend talent and I use there as anchoring , jokes , riddles and etc etc it's was in 5 std next year new night stay same friends new teacher but I don't want to do anchoring at a standard 6 and Sare log Aaye Usi Jagah per Baithe Hain Jahan per pahle Baithe the and everyone started shouting the dirgh gandhi show dirgh gandhi show that was my proud moment in new school, I am doing anchoring with my buddy Aryan after all I am dirgh One thing I get understood that

My 16th birthday party

we don't have to give up. Jis Din give up kar diya use Din Tumhari Life khatm ho jayegi Kuchh Na Kuchh life mein try karte hi Rahana chahie Nahin to life mein maja hii Nahin Hai that's all .

Abhi abhi just Meri birthday party Gayi 16th birthday party after 10 years. I have enjoyed and celebrated my birthday party and everyone was came you can see photo at this side Now I am 16. time Kitni Jaldi Chala Jata Hai like tik tik tik tik

It's been 13 days since I completed 16 years of my. exams bhi khatm ho gai hai But tension Rah raha hai mere ko result ka because my ss and Hindi paper was not good and Like I literally cry when I know that zana didn't like me and when gojo was dead and in the ending of 777 Charlie well that's all move to next chapter

Your best moment with Your mom

:–

Your best moment with Your father

:–

OFF TOPIC

Basically the of topic means I am writing this book as a way of diary. That's why this is an of topic. I am writing here date and what happened at that time 6th August my mother told me you have to come to temple at my farm. So I tell yes. She tell me we are going by walking and from my house to my farm. There is 13 km distance and I tell yes, I will come at that time friendship day was going on. So after walking 13 km my legs was paining and I go to Vishwa solanki's home first time at friendship dayFrom there I go to Eka club and from there I go to home and I want to see go for movie and my father tell bus that's all.

Your most expensive thing you have right now ?

:-

20 August ok 20 August het invited me to het home for Krishna bhagwan, celebration and yash and soyam also was invited I have watch OMG 2 , jailer movie, but I want to watch Gadar 2,so I tell to my father I want to watch gadar 2 he give me permission to watch and me and soyam decided(NY Cinemas)we don't know that NY Cinemas is very far away from het home and we book ticket. It was 450 per person.The show was at two o'clock. So we go at 12:20 it was Raining so we have borrowed het raincoat. He only have one. So soyam wear it and we go and I open Google Map It was 13 km far away from here. So slowly slowly we reach there at 1:30. We have 30

What was your best moment with your friend and worse movement with your friend?

:-

minutes more as we progress, The rain was less so our clothes were not wet and the movie was not like part 1, I didn't like it at all while going, he drive very fast. So the rainwater was inside in some rickshaw's and the rickshaw man got angry that who did this he said I said to soyam move ahead Soyam take a wrong side. So one police man catch up usne teen charges Laga Hai pahla number plate without licence and Wrong side. He was asking for 5000 rupees. So at that time we don't have any money because we pay every money for popcorn and Pepsi I tell to police man. We don't have any money if you want to check you can check soyam call her sister and ask for

FACT

The fact is everyone needs money in this world only and only money without money. There is nothing I have also spoke in the money chapter also

500 rupees so we can shut the mouth of police man, but I have manage the situation we are students. Let us go and all things emotional damage. So he tell don't do again we were okay, this police man situation was first time for me after all soyam saying Gadar 2 will be remember.and I didn't like gadar 2 at all in compare of jailer and OMG 2 I put number 1 jailer , number 2 OMG 2 and number 3 last gadar 2 that's all .

CHAPTER -4- FAMILY AND FRIENDS

I have taken friends and family together because my family is my friend and my friends are my family ohk. life mein yah donon chije To Honai Hi chahiye in my family. There are four members and plus one mama. My family is incomplete without mama. Okay. I have lots of friends, lots means lots . The most of female friends like we see on ratio 86% are female 14% male I think I have first said "dost hai tu sab ha Nahi To Kuch nahi". I think who don't have friends and family What about them? They are so sad, they don't have anyone to talk any. Okay, let's move ahead.

FATHER (PAPA)

Papa this Words, is lots for me I love my father most means in this Country and in my Whole life I Will love him most. The Best person I ever met till 16th When I Was Born He Was Sad and happy Because I Will tell that on me Section. For Him I am a King ok for him I don't think everyone Will be Exeept me As a King When Corana Was going on I Was seriously getting bored and I Want to play GTA 5 He traved HalF Ahmedabed for pS.4 So I Can play GTA 5 That's Sound so cool and he is Cool finally. He found it and buy it for me like this is only one thing. He gift me Samsung s22 phone cost 80000 (moneyfex) and etc etc he Cares a lot

For me and my brother he is the true King for me and he will be he want only one thing from me. I should have to pass on exam and I am trying my best To get best marks. Just one thing I don't like about God not papa. God means Bhagwan whom I love the most they go away from me. I can't blame to God no one can okay, forgot it my papa has liver cancer. It's true. He has only 5 years or more Doctor said that to my mother he will never tell me this I know about this one day when papa was at work. My mother called me and tell me this I was very sad at that time and I was only thinking why why means why to God whyThis is life and I have to face this now like Deepti mam, tell

at the starting of 9th from 9th , You have to face very ups and downs. You have to change your classmates and more , he is everything for me when I want To go watch movies. He let me go not when exams going on. Yeah fact hai exam ke time. No to everything. He called me dirghu it's so cute pet name for me. My papa life is not at all good. This is very complicated stories. So my grandfather has done two marriage and one more thing. My grandfather had murder someone it's very complicated. I also don't know whole story and he got punishment also 14 years jail. You can search on Google about case file Raju murder case. So my dada first wife run away

with my father sister not my father only sister. He was 14 years old. My father was alone with one worker because Dada was in jail. Dadi run away. I can't imagine my father stay alone with worker. My dada was having some loan not from Bank from different different person. So all of them come and take everything from home than worker said Please leave some plates and spoon so sir (papa) can eat food today I am eating on that plates and spoon. We did buy some new spoons We have but not plates my mota Dada give support to him. He taught him the business of agriculture now, he is the king like you can't imagine he give phone ,PS4 and more

from agriculture business. He has one more business of giving home on rent because we have one two or three flats so he give In now the best thing is when my father was getting married my dada get bal. It was a good news after this I get understood. I am very small like I am going to be 16, but in age of 14, he manage this all things.

And I can't even manage one exam. Also after all we happy in life. There is ups and downs and it will come always be happy. Like I get sad with anyone the next day. I will talk with him or her life is short. We have to enjoy everymoment. My father life is very complicated.I can't write here because it is very controversy let's move

MOM (mummy]

Okay, so mummy is not a word for me. She is everything like Jiske pass mummy nahi hoti hogi, uske upar kya Biti Hogi mere ko pata hai kya hota hai. In the starting days of Corona my mother got affected and she was hospitalised for 9 days and I knew the exact date it was 19 July because that was my brother's birthday. Okay at that time Jisko bhi corona, Hota tha vah marta tha but she successfully survive. So at that time I understood mummy Kitna Kaam karti hai yaar, Khane ki ahamiyat pata chal gayi Mummy ke Hath ka khana. me, papa and mama today also we don't know that on Tuesday which vegetables were coming in the tiffin my parents are so good. Mummy ne Aaj Tak Hath nahi Uthaya hai. Like you can see the photo in the left side. She is my mummy mere dost Kahate Hain Ki vah Tujhse Chhoti dikhti hai. Okay, I can't write more about Mummy Okay Pyar dono Ko same karta hu.

Mama (mamu)

Okay, mamu I was small when my mamu stay with us. Also like mamu is our 5th family member at now he is shifting after his marriage Mere mamu Shakuni aur kanss Jaise to bilkul Nahin Hai vah Sabse sweet hai. Aur kinds time karna Achcha lagta hai like most of people from outside thing. He is my big brother. Me and my brother and mamu also go outside for hangout and more we do lots of masti in home like I can share everything with him. He is very nice. He is very cool now he is going to leave somewhere else after marriage like my life first hangout was with him like we tell him mama so now everyone called him mama Best mamu ever I met if you are reading this I love you and you selected nice wife.

ME (DIRGH GANDHI)

Okay, so I am going age wise. So now I come my turn I was born in 2007 26th September I know time also it was 12:35 a.m. In India its called a good time for born child when I was born. I didn't cry like a baby Should have to cry But I didn't. So basically it's not a good thing for a child doctor said I drink some water from my mother stomach. So next thing I was move to another Hospital my papa was in tention because I was first na every father got tension. What will happen with me. I will die or survive he was worried about me. I tell you already I love papa most I ask to my friends give me some tag. So they give me this text.

This tags :-

1. Mastikhor
2. flutter boy
3. Maha actor
4. Best brother of 52 sister
5. Dafor boy
6. Angry one but sometimes
7. Good friend

So I didn't give this tag to me. I ask to my friends. Ok. So I do very masti when I was in second standard I started doing Masti or Masti ki kya baat karo teacher ko Tathastu bol diya tha in 3 std Flutter boy see I don't know how to do flirt vo to ho jata hai yaar, aur woh bhi only with girls and some of them enjoyed not everyone some of them, Maha actor. See I want to be a actor or director. That's

why I do lots of acting one day. I prank my friend with my acting and he was like WTF , so dafor boy I don't accept this let's go to angry one, but sometimes see so anger is your enemy, you have to control your anger. I am controlling it and always in my face there is smile. So don't get angry sometime I get because they are so dumb , best brother of 52 sister. It is true. I have 52 sister. That's why I always be nice to them sari ki sari school ki hai isliye.Good friend so they think I am good, but I am not I like to make people laugh. I am not a joker that all for me.

Like Krishna bhagwan Said yah Waqt Gujar jaega.

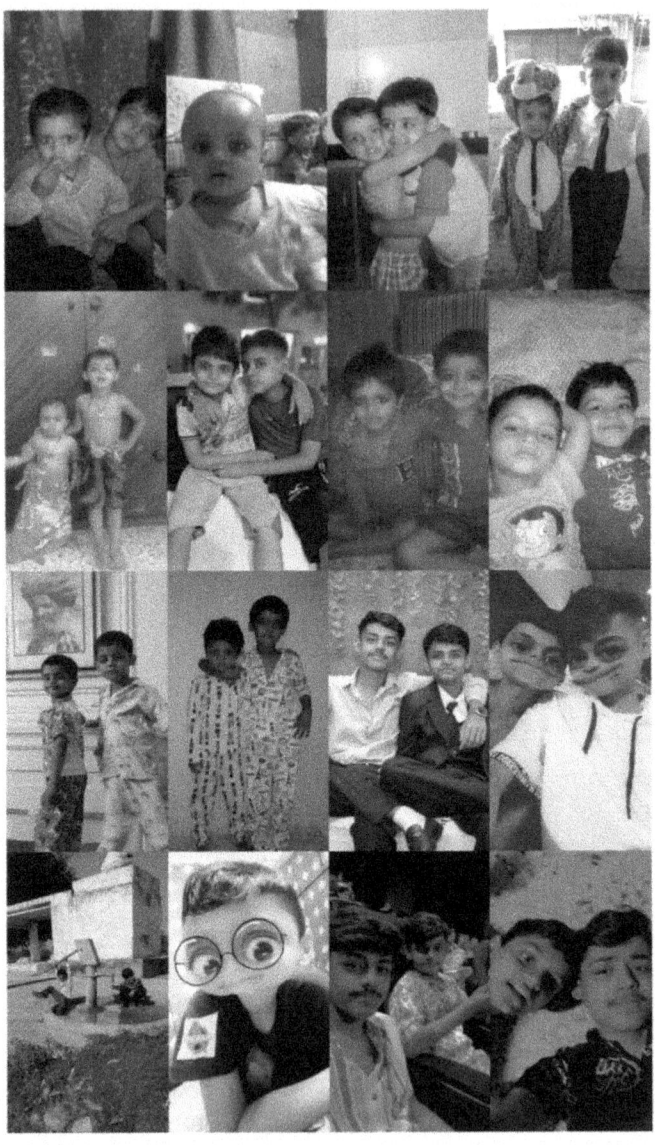

Brother (bhai)

Okay, so my brother is 3 years smaller than me chota hai mera pyara hai mere liye. I was thinking from where he come when he was born . my father And mother say that the first name he tells dirgh (egggaa) Koi To Mere ko bhai Kahane wala mil gaya, vah mere se thoda alag Hai vah Shy hai Aur Main Nahi Hoon mere ko usko Pareshan karne mein bahut maza aata hai irritation irritation and irritation Ham donon Ne bahut jhagade Kiye Hai fight a lot. We both know One thing that we can't live without each other. I don't know him but I can tell I can't live without him we have some future plans vo Thode Se Chomu Hai To Main

Nahin batane wala Ek Kadva Sach Jo Sabko accept karna hi hai mummy papa and mama Ek Din off hone wale Hain Tumko Aage iske sath hi Rahana Hai you don't know he is doing fight for PS4 or for phone or who is stronger? Basically main Hi Hoon Na stronger yaar 3 Sal Bada Ho usse vah Kabhi let go nahin karne wala hai So I have to do it. We are very cool. Just we have completed Demons slayers and we are Attacking on each other like Demons slayers fights were in a friendly way. Yeah Hai Mera Bhai thokarraj Gandhi we call him tokhar and my father name dhruv gandhi mummy ka kinjal gandhi and mama rahul vyas

FRIENDS (DOST)

Dost kya hota hai kya yah family se bhi Badhkar Hai, basically yes or no? Yes because sometimes you can't tell your parents you can't share feeling like,I like that girl. I have crush on her and that all these things you have to tell to your best friend only or normal friend Mere Ghar per Sab cool hai isliye main kah sakta hu per dusron ke ghar par nahi hota hai.And no because when your friendship is over he tells your every important secrets to everyone I have many secrets of my friends.I can expose them but I don't want to I am not like everyone to Fir Mere aur un Logon mein fark kya reh jayega. Dosti Aisi dhundho Jo Tumhari Bajaye Nahin

I have four or five best friends. My favourite best friend is Vishwas Shah I have tell her everything means everything. Soyam Patel my best friend. I know everything about him and basically I will not tell lie, but I have exposing him for one topic because I don't like that this is a little bit controversy and I will tell you but the name are wrong except soyam so High School Every boy or girl thing that they have to be in a relationship. I don't think so because I don't want to be ;I am in a relationship at a time but not now Because I was finding a girl for move on. Yeah, I know Meri Umar Kya Hai move on karne ki Tum log Yahi soch rahe hoge Move karne ki kya

Who is your favourite Best friend?

Male:-

Female :-

Umar Hai Meri so I don't want to talk. Let's move ahead There was a girl name aaaaaa..... Let's give her a name. Okay, Bhagwati we will call her (b) so my friend soyam and she was talking in call chat or offline. They both have crush on each other, but they both were not telling to each other. It's so complicated koi bhi first move karna hi nahi Chahta tha seriously dude.
At the time this was happening I was out because I don't want to participant because I don't like the girl at all and the second thing is I get some odd vibe from her and that Vibe came Truth after 1 year 5 months don't know exactly what was the date her father came means b's father (b)if you

Always make two type of friends in life
"first one like lord shri Krishna who does not fight but still make sure your victory"
And second one like karna
Who knows that defeat is in front but still does not leave your side

are reading this book sorry for this. So her father was speaking bad words to soyam in papa,mummy and else At outside of school campus. He does not have a right to speak language like this if the soyam Peacefully talking to you. I was really angry on soyam why you don't speak if he was speaking bad words you can also speak bad words because it is His fault that he spoke bad words. At that time,I was not there. So I have tell a lot to her father lot means a lot. The mistake is from both the side girl and boy So he have to scold both of them neither don't have to if there is boths fault I don't want to take it far away at the end now also, soyam talking with her as a friend

manner, but I don't think so. I always say to soyam stay away from her but he is not accepting it. I think my odd vibe is Like Deja voo I feel odd when it's not good. I tell to Vishwa Solanki don't talk with him and She talk like a friend but he propose her.

That is we are friends. We have to support our friend at the end. I have lots of friend, but I feel alone I don't know why but I that's all for this chapter. Hey, I forgot it's not the end of this chapter there is something Like I forgot to tell about malav is one of the nicest person I ever made. Bahut hi kam log Hain Jo Mere ko Hansa sakte hain aur Malav To pet Dukha Deta Hai Itna hansata hai mere ko.

I ask my friends how am I as a friend and they told?

1. dirgh Is very naughty boy he is smart, but very angry person he likes to write a book :- dhruvanshu
Dirgh is dirgh

2. Dirgh is my dumb friend he is very talkative annoying me but a good hearted :- achal

3. He is good best friend but little little annoying also far. He is always his protective and sometimes behaving over protective but little little good hearted person :- Vishwas Solanki

4. he is very good monitor in class he

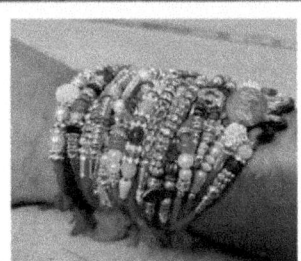

is very good at behaviour and in speech also he is monitoring at some time but doing perfectly he is good in comedy :- Pandya Vishwa .y

5. best :- Heer
6. Laughing emoji :- Krishna
7. Soooo baddddd :- megha
8. A very funny one tbh :- dharini
9. Thik par thik me bhi mazaata tere friendship ka :- Krishna

10. Very good:- HET

I have more but I am writing this only sorry who else has not been come.
:- if you want to skip my favourite you can but don't skip the last one topic

This is all my favourite. What is your favourite write here?

Ans :-

My favorite

1. Animal - rabbit, squirrel
2. Cartoon - courage the cowardly dog show
3. Movies-

action- mission impossible
Romance - Sita ram
Emotional- 777 Charlie
Sci fi - inception
Marvel - iron man
Dc - the dark knight
Friendship- Zindagi Na Milegi Dobara
Web series- Alice in Borderland
- guns and gulaabs
- cobra kai - squid game
Web move- Monica o my draling
4. vehicle - plane

5. Subject - English
6. Song - I ain't worried
          - anirudh all songs
7. Food -
Street - Pani Puri
Hotel - hocco / Chana Puri

8. Country - Japan

9. Car - Ford

10. Bike - bullet

11. Game - minecraft, gta 5

That's all I can write here

SPECIAL THANKS

:- DHARINI

:- HET SHAH

:- VISHWA SOLANKI

:- RUDRESH PANDAY

:- DHRUVANSHU

:- KATHAN GANDHI

:- VISHWA PANDEY. Y

:- SOYAM PATEL

Thank you all for supporting me for this book helping me and etc etc

LAST ONE

Finally vah page a Gaya Jab yah Kahani khatm ho jayegi aapko aapke andar vah akelapan mahsus Hoga Jaise Mere ko yah page likhate Waqt ho raha hai Nahin Bhi Ho Sakta So, thank you for supporting me. If you have any doubt you can message me on Instagram I have give a photo of my ID @yeh.dirgh if this book will be success then I will make my life till 16 part 2 because I don't Think that my life has been completed in this one book and there is one more book. I want to write Gandhi's family and second my life till 21 and lots more. Let's see what happened and in

Diwali vacationI talk with zana Basically, she was came to snap for few days and I wrote four paragraph of fullscape book at the end of Paragraph I write you have feelings for me or all over and see told me all over only two words. That's all meet...you... Soon.........

YOUR ONE AND ONLY GANDHI DIRGH GANDHI....